A PERSONAL P

PERSONAL PRAYERS
FOR
SENIORS

ALLAN W. SCHREIBER

DIMENSIONS
FOR LIVING
NASHVILLE

Good morning, dear God! Thank you for last night. Even though there are some nights when I can't sleep because my mind won't settle down or my body has some nagging aches and pains, I still want to thank you for your loving care during the night hours. Your holy angels have kept me safe.

As I begin this new day, I want to thank and praise you for giving me the wonderful assurance that I will be safe with you forever because of Jesus.

Lord, don't ever let me lose that great joy of salvation because of the pains and troubles of this life. Help me each day to say with St. Paul that the troubles and sufferings of this life are nothing compared to the great glory that we will share with our God forever.

I pray this in Jesus' name. Amen.

EVENING

The day is nearly over, Lord, and I'd like to talk with you before I go to rest.

Not everything today went as well as I wanted, so I ask for your forgiveness where I—
    hurt anyone's feelings;
    complained about all my troubles instead
    of listening to the needs of others who are
    probably suffering more than I am;
    forgot to call on you in time of need;
    failed to thank those who helped me.

Wash me clean as I go to rest tonight. It is
    wonderful to know that I can go to sleep
    in real peace, a peace that this world can
    never give. I know that if I live, I will live
    to the Lord; if I die, I will die to the Lord.

Stay with me, Lord, for your love's sake.
    Amen.

Morning

As I wake to the light of a new day, I am reminded again of those beautiful words of the psalm: "The LORD is my light and my salvation; whom shall I fear? The LORD is the stronghold of my life; of whom shall I be afraid?" (Psalm 27:1). Lord, help me walk in your light this day, so that I see your directions a little more clearly and do your will a little more faithfully.

Help me this day to—
  see the opportunities you give me for help-
    ing others;
  share the love of Jesus with those around me;
  be willing to let others help me;
  express my thanks sincerely to those who
    do for me what I can't do for myself.

If today I need to struggle with some weak-
    ness that comes as I get older, help me to
    do so with patience and without com-
    plaining.

In Jesus' precious name I pray. Amen.

One more day is over, and I am a little closer to coming home to be with you forever, dear Lord. At the end of a day it is good to reflect and count my many blessings and "name them one by one."

Thank you for the life you have given me, especially my new life in Jesus ever since my baptism. To know I am a child of God and my name is already written in the book of eternal life is the greatest comfort any person can have.

Thank you for Jesus, who gave up all his glory, humbled himself, became one of us, and obediently did God's will.

There are also many other earthly blessings that I want to remember. Thank you for my natural family, my church family, and many friends that make my short journey on this earth worthwhile. Watch over me and all my loved ones near and far, for Jesus' sake. Amen.

MORNING

Each new morning brings new opportunities, but sometimes a new day can bring fear into our hearts because we don't know how we are going to cope. At these times, Lord, help me remember the words that Moses spoke to the people of Israel as they saw the sea in front of them and Pharaoh's army coming to kill them: "Do not be afraid, stand firm, and see the deliverance that the LORD will accomplish for you today. . . . The LORD will fight for you, and you have only to keep still" (Exodus 14:13, 14).

Lord, give me faith so that I will be still and let your will be done this day in my life. No matter what happens, help me remember that in all things you are working for good to those who love you and are called by you.

Give all your people a good day, for your love's sake. Amen.

This world is hushed in darkness, and I will soon pull up the blankets and go to sleep. Please give me a sleep that is peaceful and refreshing.

Help me clear my mind of any thoughts that keep troubling me. Help me do what St. Paul encourages us all to do in Philippians 4:8, to think about "whatever is true, whatever is honorable, whatever is just, whatever is pure, whatever is pleasing, whatever is commendable."

If I do this I am sure I will sleep well tonight and feel really refreshed in the morning.

Before I go to sleep, I am thinking of my family, friends, and others who have special needs because their health is not good. Keep us all in your special care, Lord. Amen.

Thank you, Lord, for the rest you gave me last night. Today I am one day nearer to finishing the race of life and receiving the final crown of glory that has been promised to me and all believers in Christ, who has won that victory crown for us.

Praise be to you, my God, whose love over-
  shadows me every step of life's journey!
  Praise be to you, Jesus, my Lord and Savior,
  for your life, death, and resurrection, so that
  I can say with absolute certainty: Because he
  lives, I too shall live forever! Praise be to
  you, O Holy Spirit, for bringing me through
  holy baptism into God's kingdom and keep-
  ing me in true faith to this day.

Help me never to forget the importance of
  regular feeding upon your holy word and
  the precious body and blood of Jesus in
  Holy Communion.

Keep me and all my loved ones in true faith.
  Amen.

As the hymnwriter says:

"Now the day is over, night is drawing nigh,
Shadows of the evening steal across the sky."

Thank you, Lord, for hymnwriters gifted to
put down words that stay embedded in
our memory and help us express our
deeper thoughts and needs.

"Through the long night watches may thine
angels spread
Their white wings above me, watching round
my bed."

Many older people need special care during the
night. When the pains of body or mind
attack them, it seems that the night will
never come to an end. I pray for them all,
that they will find some rest and relief from
pain this night. May those who are afflicted
with terminal illness find their strength in
you. Comfort their loved ones who stand by
them, feeling so helpless at such a time. Help
us all to rely only on you at all times. Amen.

Another day has come, dear Lord. I know every day of my life is your gift to me, but sometimes when troubles pile up and the going is rough I wonder whether that gift is of much value. On such days, keep me from becoming a cynical, grumbling old grouch. Help me to see that even though life has many prickles that hurt, there are plenty of beautiful blossoms to admire, for which I must thank you, God.

I want to say thank you for—
a beautiful world in which to live;
the warmth of the sun and the refreshment of the cool breezes;
the variety of smells that give such pleasure, such as the flowers in the garden and a dinner roasting in the oven;
the loving care of my family and friends who mean so much to me in these days.

Help me show my appreciation to all who make my life not only bearable, but even enjoyable. For Jesus' sake. Amen.

At the end of a day it is good to come to you, dear God, and have a heart-to-heart talk.

First of all I want to confess that many of the good resolutions I had as I began this day were not kept as well as I hoped. Please forgive me for all the sins that have blemished my life today. It is so comforting to know that because Jesus has taken away the punishment for all sin I can go to sleep at peace with God. For those of us who are coming much closer to the end of life's journey, it is so important to have the confidence that whether we live or whether we die, we are the Lord's.

I pray for all those who do not have that confidence. Open the door for them to come to know Jesus as Lord and Savior, so they can enjoy life as God has planned for us. Help me or some other Christian friend to lead them to meet Jesus.

Give me a good sleep now, for Jesus' sake. Amen.

MORNING

As I draw closer to the end of life, most days are still very fruitful and some are very exciting, but there are some that are rather uninteresting. Lord, please keep from me the spirit of complaining, because I know that such a spirit robs me of the joy of life and makes me almost unbearable to others.

Help me this day to—
remember to thank you for all the little
pleasures of life;
try to discover and do your good will;
avoid any conflicts with family or friends;
bite my tongue when I am tempted to
criticize;
show the love of Jesus just a little better.

Lord, it is so easy to make all these good resolutions in this time of prayer, but so difficult to remember them during the day. Help me to do them, and forgive me when I forget. In Jesus' name I pray. Amen.

Thanks for all you have done to make this a good day for me, dear Lord. When I think of my failures and mistakes, I certainly do not deserve all you have done for me, but I know how full of love and generosity you are. Help me to be filled with your Spirit, so that I can be just as loving and gracious to those around me.

I am sorry for those times this day when—
  I was impatient with others or myself;
  I failed to help others;
  I talked too much instead of listening for
    the needs of others;
  I gave the devil any opportunity to lead me
    astray.

Let me hear those beautiful words: "Your sins
    are forgiven, in the name of the Father
    and of the Son and of the Holy Spirit."

Refresh me, Lord, with sweet sleep, so that when
    I wake I can do what you want me to do to
    the best of my God-given ability. Amen.

Morning

As I awake each morning, the thought runs through my mind: Well, you have allowed me to live another day here on earth.

Dear God, I do feel sorry for those people who do not have Jesus as the Lord of their lives. If you give me the chance today to tell anyone about how you love and save us, help me have the courage and the wisdom to say the right words at the right time. I know you want all people to come to know the truth and be saved.

When I was younger I thought it would be easier for older people to realize the importance of having the assurance of eternal life with God, but there are many of my age group who don't want to think about what happens after we die. Lord, you love them as much as you love me, so break down their resistance to your great love, so that they can have eternal life. For Jesus' sake I pray. Amen.

Lord, when we come to the sunset years of life, we realize that there is not a lot more for us to accomplish before our last day comes.

For whatever I have been able to achieve this day, I want to give you thanks. Help me feel a sense of achievement from even the little things I am able to do each day. Keep from my mind those depressing thoughts that can make me feel worthless or useless.

As I go to rest tonight, fill my mind with good thoughts. I want to remember that you are my creator and you think I am worthwhile. You loved me with the greatest possible love by giving your own Son to sacrifice his life so that I will never be separated from you.

This is all I need as I end this day: Jesus, only Jesus! Amen.

Lord Jesus, you have given us so much wisdom through your words. We can never come to understand fully all you have said, but this morning I want to thank you that by the power of your living word I have come to know the truth about how life is meant to be lived on this earth. Don't ever let me be tempted away from the regular daily meditation on your word and the regular worship in God's house.

Let your Holy Spirit join with my spirit each day to remind me that I am God's precious child.

Whatever I have to do this day, give me the strength to do it well, so that when I come to the evening I can feel it was a good day.

Be with all who will suffer pain or grief this day. Give them strength to bear the troubles of life. Hear my prayer for your love's sake. Amen.

There are times when it is difficult to cope with the troubles that come because of the weaknesses of old age. When I am troubled, make me humble enough to accept the help that others want to give me.

If others are suffering, help me be willing to reach out with a helping hand, as Jesus did when he was here on earth with us.

When family or friends are struggling with conflicts, help me to be a gentle peace-maker, so that the spirit of love can be restored.

Thank you, Lord, for all the good things that happened today, and forgive me for anything that I messed up. Give me a restful sleep. Amen.

MORNING   Day 9

As I begin this new day, I want to thank you for the rest you gave me last night, and to think about the blessings of life I enjoy through the fellow members of my church family.

Thank you for the pastor who leads the worship and feeds me with God's word and the Lord's Supper, for those who provide the music to lead our worship, for those who help meet the needs of fellow members, for those who visit the lost or wandering, and for those who help the young grow up as disciples of Jesus.

Without my church family, my life would be very different and so much the poorer. Help me do my share of your work, Lord, so that I will feel useful even to the very end of this life.

In Jesus' name I pray. Amen.

It is a good feeling to come to the end of the day, to relax, and to look forward to a good sleep.

Tonight, Lord, I want to say thanks for the many pleasures of life that you have given us—music, books, films, adventures in sight-seeing, the company of family and loving friends.

When the time comes that I can no longer enjoy all these pleasures, help me not to feel cheated or bitter, and not to blame you, but to remember all the blessings you have given me and still provide.

Be with those who will not sleep very well tonight because of pain or any other distress. Keep us in your loving care until the fever of this life is over and we are home at last. Amen.

Good morning, Lord! It is said that as people grow older they grow in wisdom. Help me live in such a way that any wisdom I have been given may be of value to other people. Grant me above all the wisdom that helps me grow in a right relationship with you.

I am reminded how this life is like waiting for the bridegroom Jesus Christ to return. I remember how Jesus told us to be wise, like the five wise bridesmaids who not only waited for the bridegroom to return, but took enough oil so that their lamps would be burning brightly when he returned. Help me to have this wisdom.

By the power of your Holy Spirit, keep my love relationship with you shining brightly every day, until at last I can join with all your saints as we cry out: "Here is the bridegroom! Come out to meet him."

Come soon, Lord Jesus! Amen.

Another day has come to an end, and Jesus has not yet returned.

Thank you, Lord, for the gift of life. As I find good things to enjoy, I give you praise. Where I did anything today that made life difficult for others, please forgive me. When life holds sorrow, pain, grief, or tears, help me be aware of your special comfort.

At such times, turn me to your word, to prayer, to the fellowship and support of fellow members of my church family. I know how easy it is to want to hide in my own shell and brood over my sorrows. Help me be willing to let others serve me in my times of need, and then I will be even better able to help them in their needs.

Let your love flow into me and out to others, all through this day. I pray in the name of him who is love, Jesus our Lord. Amen.

God, be with me all through this day.
Be in my mind and in all my thinking.
Be in my words and all my speaking.
Be in my heart and all my loving.
Be in my spirit so that all I do this day will
be pleasing to you and helpful to all I
meet.

I want to spend a few moments praying for
those who are facing difficulties in life—
the sick and dying, the terminally ill,
especially those who have great pain, the
bereaved who feel the loss of loved ones,
the handicapped, the unemployed, and
all who feel life is not easy.

Help me and others to take time to help those
in need by making a visit or a telephone
call. May the great love of Jesus shine
through us and reach the lives of others. I
pray in his name. Amen.

At times, Lord, I hear myself and others of the older generation say how bad the world is becoming. We tend to look back and call the past "the good old days." It is easy to sit back and be very critical, but I want to get beyond criticism. I realize that I too am partly responsible that this present world is not as good as it should be.

Even though I may not be in a position of
     great influence, give me wisdom to help
     those around me, especially the younger
     people, to realize that this world becomes
     a much better place to live in when we let
     God be our God and Jesus be our Savior
     and Lord. Then the great love that our
     God gives will fill our lives and flow into
     the world to make it even better than "the
     good old days."

I end this prayer with a confident Amen, yes,
     it shall be so.

My Lord, what a morning! On some mornings I wonder how the night went so quickly, but there are other mornings when I am pleased to see that the daylight has come and the long night hours of waiting for morning are over. Whenever sleepless nights come, help me find some useful things to do without disturbing others, instead of just lying in bed becoming more and more frustrated and depressed.

As this new day begins, I am reminded of your promise that there will be a final new day when darkness will cover the earth, and we shall see Jesus return with all the angels and archangels in a glory too bright for these old earthly eyes to behold. We shall all be caught up to meet him in the air, changed to a wonderful new creation forever.

Help us keep our anticipation for that great day strong and bright, so that we can share it with others who may feel that there is no eternal hope.

Help me to do this each day, for Jesus' sake. Amen.

Lord Jesus, you are our God, the same yester-
day, today, and forever. The world around us is
in constant change, and I wonder how much
of that change is for the better and how much
is no good at all. It isn't always easy for those
of us who are older in years to cope with dra-
matic changes. But I do ask you to help me
keep an open mind, so that I don't simply
condemn all the changes.

Help me be positive, so that I can enjoy the
    changes that can be useful, and give me
    courage to give a loving warning when I
    can see clearly where changes are going to
    cause terrible trouble for your people.

Once again, I thank you that you do not
    change—your love, mercy, forgiveness,
    promises, faithfulness, and all your gifts
    will never fail.

All thanks and praise to you, O God. Amen.

Morning

Dear Lord, the longer I live, the more I have to praise and adore you for the wonderful way you made us and the tremendous enjoyments there are for us here on this earth. Today I want to think about the necessity and pleasure of food. You have asked us to pray for our daily bread, and I know how well you do provide for us day by day.

You could have given us a small variety of food that would keep us healthy, but in your generosity you have given us an end-less variety to enjoy. And then we can enjoy all this food with family and friends, which adds to our earthly pleasure.

I can enjoy so much, but I want to pray also for those who live in places where there are droughts and famines. Help me see ways that I can help make life more bear-able for any who are starving or suffering.

I pray in Jesus' holy name. Amen.

Lord, as I look back on the day just gone, I am again troubled that I did not reflect your great qualities like love, patience, peace, faithfulness, and kindness as well as I wanted to. Please forgive me and give me an even greater measure of your Spirit, so that I can still grow to be a little more like the person you want me to be.

If others have reason to correct me, please help me receive such correction without resentment. If there has been any upset in a relationship between me and a family member or friend, help me speak words of peace and forgiveness before this day ends.

Each day many people are hurt through unkind words, thoughtless actions, physical violence, accidents, hatred, and open warfare. Comfort them and their loved ones, and lead others who are filled with your love to reach out and help to heal them.

May your holy angels watch over us all as we rest tonight. Amen.

As long as we live we are facing a battle. In our physical life there is the battle to survive each day, and in our spiritual life there is the battle against the devil, the world around us, and our old sinful nature.

As far as physical life is concerned, I am not greatly concerned whether it lasts one year or ten years. I do pray that my last days will not be filled with great pain, and that I may breathe my last in peace with you, my God, so that I can be at home forever.

As I think about the battle in my spiritual life, I ask for the complete armor you have given me to wear—the belt of truth, the breastplate of righteousness, my feet fitted with readiness that comes from the good news of peace, the shield of faith, the helmet of salvation, and the sword of the Spirit which is the word of God. Help me use this armor so that the evil one will never gain the victory over me. In Jesus' name. Amen.

It is important for me at the end of each day to come to you as a child comes to a father and tell you what happened during the day.

Some things went very well, just as I had planned. Other things did not turn out so well, and I have to confess that much of the problem was me. Please forgive me and give me encouragement to keep up the efforts to make improvements.

Very often those improvements I look for are slow in coming, and I am tempted to give up hope. If I have been difficult to live with today, by being irritable, bad-tempered, unwilling to see any other's point of view, or failing to keep any promises I made, please forgive me.

I know I am washed clean in the precious blood of Jesus my Savior and my Lord. In his name I pray. Amen.

At the beginning of this new day I want to give thanks for times of celebration. I think of all the celebrations we enjoy as we remember what you, our God, have done for us. I remember the celebration of Christmas, as we rejoice that you came to live with us. Then I think of your great sacrifice for all our sin on Good Friday and the wonderful joy of Easter, as we see how you conquered sin and death once and for all.

I thank you for the marvelous gift of your Holy Spirit after Jesus returned to his heavenly throne. By his power I have been made a child of God.

Thank you also for the celebrations I can enjoy with many friends and family members: birthdays, weddings, wedding anniversaries, dinners, and barbecues. Let all celebrations be a reminder for me to look forward each day to the final celebration of glory in a new heaven and earth forever. Amen.

Before I go to rest, I come to you, my God, to express my thanks for all your love and kindness. When Jesus was on earth as one of us, he often experienced our human ingratitude. I remember the story when he cured ten lepers and only one came back to say thank you.

Tonight I want to express my thankfulness
  for at least some of the great blessings you
    give me each day—
  for life itself, so that I can enjoy each day
    as it comes;
  for the gift of your eternal kingdom; for my
    loved ones in my family, who give me so
    much love and joy;
  for friends both within and beyond my
    church family, whose company adds so
    much to the pleasure of life;
  for the energy and abilities to work and do
    things that give me a sense of satisfaction.

When I forget to be thankful, please forgive
  me. Amen.

During this early part of the day I want to say thank you for last night's sleep, and I want to talk to you a little about the passing of time.

As I grow older, I realize more clearly that my time on earth is running out. Some people I know simply ignore this fact, and others don't want to think about it because it makes them feel depressed.

Those of us who know and worship you are not worried that our earthly time may soon be over. Our hearts are not earth-bound but heaven-centered, and so we wait with excitement for the future time when all God's people of all nations will be united in glory with the triune God forever.

Help me make the best use of the time I still have to work before the end of my time comes, especially by sharing the love of Jesus with others. I pray in his name. Amen.

At the end of some days I have a feeling of real satisfaction because I have been able to do almost everything I planned, but there are some days when I feel very frustrated and disappointed because I couldn't work as quickly as I had hoped and there were many interruptions. Help me at such times to have a good sense of humor, to be able to laugh at myself and my weaknesses, and keep away from me all anger and bitterness.

Lord, I want to plan wisely and do the best I can each day, but let me be flexible so that I can say cheerfully: "What I didn't get done today, I can do tomorrow or some other time." Then I know that I will not be adding unnecessary stress to my life.

Take away all the tension from my mind and body, and let me sleep in peace. May the God of peace preserve us blameless to the coming of our Lord Jesus Christ. Amen.

Lord, it is good to wake up in the morning and remember that by your gift I am a member of your kingdom. However, I want to be more than just a member of that wonderful kingdom; I want to keep growing in the kind of life that kingdom people are to live.

Help me today to grow in the gift of faith. On many occasions Jesus said "Fear not" or "Do not worry." He told us to consider the birds that fly around and never store up any food and yet our heavenly Father feeds them all.

I must confess that the birds have a much greater trust than I do. Forgive me, Lord, for my lack of trust, and help me live without hoarding things that I will probably never use. Help me be more generous in giving things away when I see the needs of others. Let me be satisfied with the simple necessities of life.

For Jesus' sake I pray. Amen.

At the close of another day, when my body is weary and I look for rest, it is good to be still and know that you are my God.

I confess that in the course of the day there
were many times when I forgot to think
about you, Lord, but it is not easy to keep
you in mind all the time, because I am
concentrating on work I'm doing and you
are not visibly present to make me aware
that you are all around me.

Forgive me all the sins of the past day.
Remind me again that I can be absolutely
sure that all my sins are forgiven and I do
have eternal life because your Son Jesus
has lived a perfect life in my place, has
suffered all the punishment of sin for me,
and has risen from the dead to guarantee
that peace with God has been restored
forever.

In that assurance let me go to sleep. Amen.

As I set out on the journey of a new day, Lord, I want to listen and talk to you. I want to hear your directions for me as I live today according to your word.

Your word tells me that the blessed person is one who not only listens to your directions, but also delights in doing your will and meditates on your law day and night. If you help me do this regularly, then I too will be like a tree planted by streams of water, bearing wonderful fruit in my life.

Without Jesus, none of these things would ever be possible for me, because my sin would be a barrier blocking me from the great love of God. Thank you again, dear Jesus, for your sacrifice, the pain and agony you endured to set me and all people free from the curse of sin and death.

Let me show in my life today how much I love you and all people. Amen.

Now it is time to rest beneath night's shadow. It is time to offload all the problems and worries of life, and commit myself into your loving care, heavenly Lord. But when I read or watch the news I don't find it easy to get rid of all the stress of life. We hear reports from all over the world of strife, war, earthquakes, floods, fires, and famines. As a result of all these calamities, people are dying, and there is a flood of tears as the people of this earth cry out in personal pain or mourn the loss of loved ones.

I know that the pain and tears of your people will not cease until you take them home with you, but in the meantime have pity on us and relieve our pain and sorrow. Help us convey your great love to one another, so that we may experience your comfort flowing among us more each day.

Give me that same comfort as I go to sleep this night, for Jesus' sake. Amen.

As I make plans for a new day, I sometimes wonder whether much of what I do is simply my own plan and not really what you, my Lord, would like me to do. Help me this day and every day to examine my plans and to make sure I am not simply doing what pleases me. It is so easy for me to avoid those things that are more difficult, like making time to visit the lonely, or doing some jobs for someone who needs help.

Help me realize that even if I do some of the more difficult work, my tasks are easy compared to all you did for me, to give me the great joy of life both now and forever.

Fill me with your Spirit, so that I may truly reflect the great love and joy that you have given me. Help me to see and take any opportunity you give to explain the hope that is in me through Jesus Christ alone. Amen.

The day is almost over. Each day I read of many who have passed through the valley of the shadow of death. One day my name will appear on that list of the departed, and I will leave behind my loved ones and friends.

Heavenly Lord, you have given us only one life
to live, and then after death comes the judg-
ment. I think of those wonderful words of
Simeon: "Master, now you are dismissing
your servant in peace, according to your
word; for my eyes have seen your salvation."

All praise be to you, dear God, that I can pray
those words of Simeon because I know
Jesus, the only Savior. I am so grateful that
my salvation does not depend on how well
I have lived, but I do want to show my
gratitude for that gift by doing what is best.

Forgive me when I give in to temptation and
fall into sin. Wash me and I will be clean.
I pray in the name of Jesus. Amen.

In this morning hour I come to you, my Lord, looking for your instructions as I continue my journey of life. In Psalm 32 you said: "I will instruct you and teach you the way you should go; I will counsel you with my eye upon you" (v. 8).

You also remind me not to be like a horse or a mule which has to be controlled by bit and bridle. Give me a mind that is open to understand your good will for me this day, and take away any selfishness or stubbornness that might spoil a good day.

When I do make mistakes, make me wiling to confess them instead of trying to make excuses, and then to ask for forgiveness from you and from those I hurt. Then I will have true blessedness, because all my sins are covered. I pray through Jesus, whose blood cleanses me from all sin. Amen.

It is really comforting to come to the end of a day knowing that our God has the whole world in his hands.

During the day we hear sirens of ambulances on their way to road accidents, of police cars on their way to deal with law-breakers. We watch television and see the terrible effects of wars and famine. Lord, there is so much tragedy and heartache in this world. I long for the fulfillment of your promise when there will be a new heaven and a new earth where there will be no more death or crying or pain.

This world will surely pass away. So while I still have to live here, help me never become too attached to the material things I have collected over the years. When my time comes to depart and be with Christ, help me see that nothing on this earth can compare with the great glory you have in store for us. In Jesus' saving name I pray. Amen.

Dear Lord, as I begin this new part of life's journey, I want to thank you that in my baptism you adopted me as your child.

Thank you for my parents and all who have helped me grow in a loving relationship with you, especially those in my church family who worship with me and pray for me.

As I meet people in the world, I find so many who say there is no God or who say that God will just let everyone enter heaven because he is so kind. I know that your word is truth, and Jesus said that he is the only way to you.

I pray for your Holy Spirit to open the minds of those who are lost from God, so that they too can enjoy life now and forever.

Keep me and all your people safe this day. Amen.

Evening

It is good to be home safe at the end of a day. Thank you, Lord, for your protection from all dangers, both physical and spiritual.

I know that the old evil foe tries hard to get me away from Jesus and the assurance of eternal life with God. Help me remember that I need the great power of the Holy Spirit to keep the faith right to the very end.

It is your word and the Lord's Supper that keep me in true faith, so help me and all the people of God to use these gifts faithfully.

Forgive me all the sins of today. Watch over me, my loved ones, my friends, and all people this night.

My soul finds rest in you alone, my God. You alone are my rock and my salvation. Amen.

As we come toward the end of life's journey, many of us struggle with a variety of physical problems. I pray this morning especially for those who are no longer able to move around.

It is not easy to be always depending on other people to move from place to place. Heavenly Lord, provide for them plenty of helpers and lots of patience when they have to wait for help to come. Keep from their hearts all frustration and any bitterness that might put their relationship with you in danger.

Fill me and all your people with the gifts of your Spirit, so that we can become better disciples of our Lord and be better able to keep doing the work he has given us to do until the end comes and our work is done.

I pray all this for your great love's sake. Amen.

Lord, your word to us is full of many promises. The promise that I want to remember this night is: "If we confess our sins, he who is faithful and just will forgive us our sins and cleanse us from all unrighteousness" (1 John 1:9).

Where I have not done my best, or where I have hurt anyone during this day, please forgive me. I have to confess that even though my old nature has been drowned ever since my baptism, it still troubles me every day, and often I make the same mistakes.

I do appreciate your forgiveness, but help me also to overcome my weaknesses.

It is good to go to rest at night knowing that I have peace with my God through the forgiveness of sins. All this is possible because of my Lord Jesus, in whose name I pray. Amen.

Dear God, you are love, and as I start a new day I want to abide in you and the great love you give me. Help me pass a little more of your love around among the people I meet today.

Help me recognize the good things others do, and be ready to give a compliment and a word of praise.

Where people are facing troubles or difficulties, help me show sympathy and give a word of encouragement.

If someone offends me, help me be quick in offering forgiveness. When things don't happen as quickly as I would like, give me patience, and remind me that I am not as young as I used to be. So help me today to be helpful to all I meet and, if possible, to hurt no one. For Jesus' sake. Amen.

As I go to sleep, I ask that you will renew the strength of my tired body for what I have to do tomorrow. I am often amazed that there is always so much to do each day. I also realize that one day I will not be here to do all those jobs, and someone else will have to do them.

What I look forward to most of all is to hear you, my Lord, say: "Well done, good and faithful servant." Where I have not been as good and faithful as I should have been, please forgive me.

As I lie down this night, relax any tensions of my body and mind. If there are any pains that are troubling me, please give me relief so I can have a good rest.

Be with all your people, so that we can lie down with the assurance of your protection. In the name of Jesus, I ask all these things. Amen.

Lord, there are some people who feel that old age has made them rather useless. This morning I want to remember your word that says the righteous are like trees planted in the house of the Lord, that still bear fruit in old age and are always green and strong. Because of Jesus I know that I can be counted as one of the righteous, and so I ask you to help me keep bearing fruit to the very end of my life.

Help me never to feel useless because I am older. Help me realize that my experience can be helpful to those who follow after me. I pray that something of what I do will make the world a little better, at least for a few people.

Give me, at the end of this day, a sense of satisfaction that my efforts were worthwhile. In all I do, may others see that I try to do what is pleasing to God. In Jesus' name I pray. Amen.

There is no such thing as a perfect day, but some days are better than others. Thank you for today, for what it was with all its ups and downs.

As the day ends, I want to thank you, my Lord, for your great love and continual forgiveness. Thank you for giving me and all your people the assurance that your mercy, patience, love, and kindness never end.

Forgive me if today I have behaved badly or if I acted hastily without considering the feelings of others. May the precious blood of Jesus wash me clean, so that I have the wonderful assurance that I am right with God as I go to rest this night.

I know I can pray all this confidently in the name of Jesus. Amen.

Lord, I want to enjoy this new day as best I can. As we grow older, we give much more thought to what we can and what we can't do. As we face each day, we remember your word that tells us that the length of our days is seventy years—or eighty, if we have strength; yet their span is but trouble and sorrow, for they quickly pass, and we fly away.

I realize full well that one day I too shall be among the forgotten dead, but that does not make me feel sad. Every Sunday I confess with absolute confidence that I believe in the resurrection of the body and the life everlasting.

My Lord Jesus, you have gone ahead as the first fruit of all who will rise, to prepare a place for all believers. Praise to you for the privilege of being among that chosen number. Now I will surely enjoy today in your company. Amen.

Dear God, I thank you for today. Thank
you—
   for the health and strength to do the things
      I wanted to do;
   for my loved ones and friends who love
      me, care for me, and pray for me;
   for the times you helped me to overcome
      any temptation;
   most of all for Jesus and his tremendous
      love for me.

I can now go to rest in the comfort that you
      have forgiven all my sins.

Help me show how grateful I am for all these
      gifts—by growing in love and obedience
      to you, in service to others, and in gen-
      erosity to all people, to give as you have
      given so generously to me.

Give me a refreshing sleep and a good day
      tomorrow. I pray in Jesus' name. Amen.

Before I go to do what I have planned today, I want to pray for others who are less fortunate than I am. I think of those who in their last years have lost their eyesight or hearing, for whom life is now very difficult.

I pray for those who have lost the ability to think clearly and to remember, who can no longer remember even their loved ones. I think of all who are feeling very lonely.

Give all these needy people the love and care of family and many friends.

If I meet any of these people in need today, help me be like the good Samaritan and put aside my own work and plans to give them something of the love you have already given to me. Help me be a little more like Jesus. Amen.

It seems that these days I spend quite a lot of time waiting. I wait for medical treatment, for public transport, and for important things to happen. As I wait I am reminded of Simeon, who was promised that before he died he would see the promised Savior. After he saw the child Jesus he spoke those wonderful words: "Lord, now you are dismissing your servant in peace . . . for my eyes have seen your salvation."

Thank you, Lord, that I don't have to wait for
    your salvation. I can join with Simeon
    and confess that I have seen your salva-
    tion. Thank you, Jesus, that you have
    done everything to make me right with
    God. Thank you, Holy Spirit, that by your
    gift of faith I can enjoy real life with God.

There is only one important waiting period
    left, and then I will meet my Lord face-to-
    face. Then I will be home at last. Amen.

What will a day bring? Even though I have made plans for this day, I know that all things are in your hands, dear Lord in heaven. It is good to know the promise of your word that assures me that all things work for good to those who love you.

But some of the things that happen don't seem good at all. At those times, give me extra faith to believe that even though things don't look good at the moment, there is a good purpose for them all.

Maybe I'll see the reason for some things that happen only after this life is over, but I know you do love me, and that's all that counts.

Help me grow closer to my Lord, so that I can understand how it is in losing myself in him that I gain the life that is best. This I ask in Jesus' name. Amen.

EVENING

At night when it is dark enough, one can see the stars. When I look at this world that you gave us, Lord, there certainly is plenty of darkness. As I watch television and read the newspapers, my heart bleeds, and I know your heart bleeds too, for the millions who suffer because of the greed and selfishness of other people.

In this darkness, help all your people to keep their eyes fixed on the Star of Bethlehem and see Jesus, who is the one remaining hope for ourselves and our faltering world. Help us be wise like those wise men of old who saw his star in the east and came to worship. When they saw the child, they worshiped him with the offering of their gifts, and then departed on another way home.

Let me keep worshiping my Savior with all I am and have, and then I will depart on the way to my heavenly home. For Jesus' sake. Amen.

Let all I do be done with thanksgiving. Lord, there is no better way to begin a new day— even if the sun refuses to break through the cloud cover, or if the problems to be faced in the coming hours appear too great to bear. It is surely my privilege and need to begin each day with true thankfulness.

I know that the greatest reason for this is the wonderful generosity of my God given to me and all people in Jesus. I am sure my sins are forgiven. I am a saint of God, covered with the beautiful garment of Jesus and all he has done for me.

With such confidence and thankfulness I can step boldly into this new day, able to face any circumstances, to reflect the love of God even in the darkest and most difficult hours that might come my way. I can do all things through Christ who strengthens me. Amen.

At the end of a day it is good to come before you, my God, with all openness and honesty. Ever since we fell into sin, we humans have become experts in trying to hide our real selves from you and from one another. Maybe I can succeed in hiding my real self from other people, but I know that you know all about me. There are no secrets between you and me. At first that makes me a little afraid that you might reject me, but then I remember how you have shown us your great love, patience, mercy, and forgiveness.

You have given us Jesus, your only Son, so
   that we can have the absolute assurance
   of eternal life with you.

Take away all the guilt of this past day. Make
   me clean as the holy, precious blood of
   Jesus washes away all my sin. Now I will
   sleep in your peace. Amen.

MORNING

Lord, you created us male and female so that we could marry, have children, and enjoy the blessings of family life. Today I want to pray for all who have promised faithfulness in marriage. Help them work hard at making their marriage and family pleasing to you and happy for each other.

Around us we see so many broken marriages and divided families. I pray especially for those who are near and dear to me, that they will realize that the love needed for life and marriage comes from God who is love.

When troubles do come, help us all to turn to you, and to strong, caring, Christian friends who will support us all the way through the troubled times. Keep us from selfishness that wants to find an easy way out, and help us be willing to work hard with great love and patience to find a God-pleasing solution. In Jesus' loving name I pray. Amen.

Day follows after day, and night after night. This world just keeps going on, and we keep going with it until we come to the end of life's journey. There is no way for us to stop the world so that we can get off for a while.

Sometimes when I see the tragedies of life, the hustle and bustle, the frantic search for security in money and material things of life, and all the dangers that surround us, I feel like praying that the world would stop.

There is a danger for us who are older to try to reach back into the "good old days" and hang on with all our might to past ways. We would like to impose these on the younger generation. Help us, Lord, to find our security not in the past but only in following you. Let me take your hand anew this night, and hold me tightly so that I keep moving forward with you. Amen.

When days are good, there are many people who do not bother to think about God and the real meaning of life. Then when troubles come, we hear them complain about how badly God is treating them. It is easy for me to condemn such people, but today I don't want to do that. I pray that in the hard times these people might be led by your Spirit to think a little more about the meaning of life and to see their need to have a relationship of love with God.

Help me be wiling to go down into the dark
   valleys with others and bring to them the
   love and healing of Christ. I pray especially for those near to me who have wan-
   dered away from you. May the detour
   they have taken lead them back home to
   you. Then we will rejoice with all the
   angels over those who were lost but now
   are found.

I pray for your great love's sake. Amen.

This evening, Lord, I want to thank you that you have taken my hand and led me over life's rough way, and with heavenly manna have fed me day by day.

I enjoy the privilege of feeding upon your holy word. I love to come often to the Lord's Supper and commune with my Lord and his people. I enjoy this daily talk in prayer. It is so good to meet with fellow members of the body of Christ in fellowship and the study of God's word, and to work as a team in doing the work you have given us to do.

If I have spoiled life for anyone today because I spoke out of turn or was too critical or failed to give help when it was needed, please forgive me. Keep me from judging and make me slow to criticize. Help me to love intensely, forgive always, and live sacrificially. For Jesus' sake. Amen.

One might think that when we come nearer to the end of life we would be very mature people. Our physical life certainly matures very naturally, but it is sad to see older people who have not matured spiritually with God. When things aren't done their way we hear their cries like little children who throw temper tantrums.

Dear God, when I hear Jesus call me to deny myself, take up the cross and follow him, and when he calls me to think first of others and serve them with great generosity of time, effort, and money, help me show maturity as a disciple of my Lord. Let me be willing to be a servant and not to count the cost.

May I reflect and transmit to others something of the great love and sacrifice that has touched my life through Jesus Christ. Amen.

When we come home at evening we sometimes ask a friend or family member: How was your day? Thank you for a good day today, Lord.

Not everything went as smoothly as I would
   have liked, and I didn't do your will as
   well as I had hoped. But I thank you for
   the good things I enjoyed, and I ask your
   pardon for anything I may have spoiled.

As I review my life, I realize that the small
   part I play will have no earth-shattering
   results in the course of history, but I know
   that you love me dearly. I can go to rest
   knowing that you consider me a very special person. Your word promises me that I
   belong to your chosen people, the royal
   priesthood of all believers, a holy nation,
   a people belonging to God.

Your Spirit has testified with my spirit that I
   am your child. Now I can rest with Jesus
   in true peace. Amen.

PERSONAL PRAYERS FOR SENIORS

Copyright © 1992 Lutheran Publishing House, © 1995 Openbook Publishers, 205 Halifax Street, Adelaide, South Australia
American edition published 2002 by Dimensions for Living

This book is printed on recycled, acid-free, elemental-chlorine–free paper.

Library of Congress Cataloging-in-Publication Data

Schreiber, Allan W.
    Personal prayers for seniors / Allan W. Schreiber.
        p. cm.—(A personal prayer book)
    ISBN 0-687-05244-0 (alk. paper)
    1. Aged—Prayer-books and devotions—English.   2. Prayers.
        I Title.   II. Series.

BV4580 .S323 2002
242'.85—dc21

                                                    2001056181

Scripture quotations are from the New Revised Standard Version of the Bible copyright © 1989 by The Division of Christian Education of The National Council of the Churches of Christ in the USA.

02 03 04 05 06 07 08 09 10 11—10 9 8 7 6 5 4 3 2 1

MANUFACTURED IN THE UNITED STATES OF AMERICA